SPECTRUM®
READERS

LEVEL 1

ALERT!

Wild Weather

By Katharine Kenah

Carson-Dellosa
Publishing

SPECTRUM

An imprint of Carson-Dellosa Publishing, LLC
P.O. Box 35665
Greensboro, NC 27425-5665

carsondellosa.com

Printed in the USA. All rights reserved.
ISBN 978-1-62399-139-5

01-002131120

Weather is all around you.
Some weather is hot.
Some weather is cold.
And some weather is wild!

Storm Cloud

This is a storm cloud. Storm clouds are filled with drops of water.

Lightning

This is lightning.
Lightning flashes in the sky.

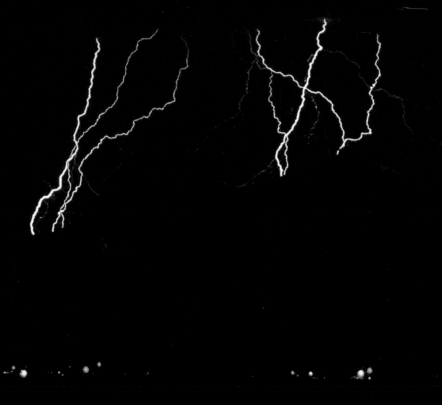

Rain

This is rain.
Drops of water
fall from a cloud.

Flood

This is a flood.
Too much rain
brings a flood.

Drought

This is a drought.
Too little rain makes
a drought.

Dust Storm

This is a dust storm.
Dust storms fill the
air with dirt and sand.

Fog

This is fog.
Fog is a cloud that
is on the ground.

Rainbow

This is a rainbow. Rainbows are made when the sun shines through raindrops.

Hail

This is hail.
Hail is made of
tiny balls of ice.

Snow

This is snow.
No two snowflakes
are the same.

Ice Storm

This is an ice storm.
Ice covers everything!

Tornado

This is a tornado.
Tornados are storms
with very strong winds.

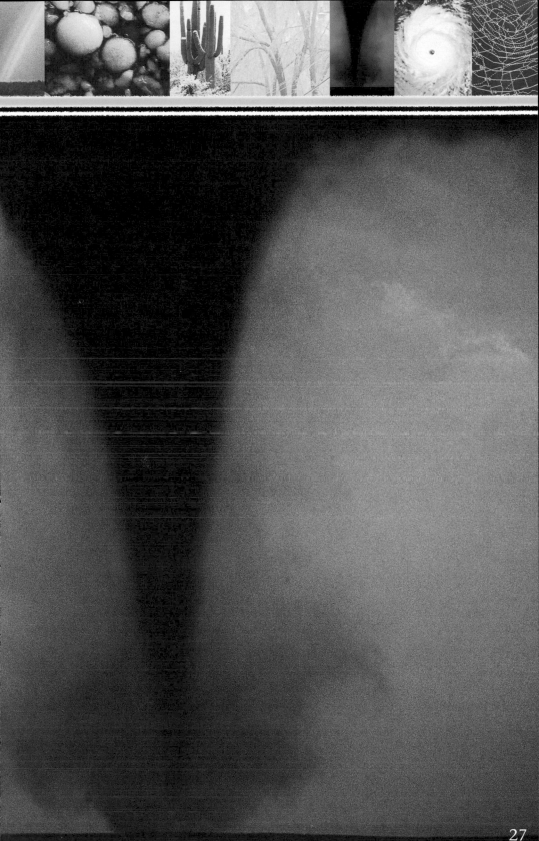

Hurricane

This is a hurricane.
Hurricanes are big
storms from the sea.

Weather Service

This is the weather service. The weather service tells you when the weather will be wild!

ALERT! Wild Weather Comprehension Questions

1. When are you most likely to see lightning?

2. Why is rain a good thing? When can it be a bad thing?

3. What causes a flood?

4. What causes a drought?

5. What is fog?

6. Can you name the colors in a rainbow?

7. When might you see a rainbow?

8. In which season are you most likely to see hail?

9. What is a tornado? Use two words to describe a tornado.

10. What is the weather like today? Use two words to describe it.